D1716810

Managing Your Weight with Nutrition

Mason Crest
450 Parkway Drive, Suite D
Broomall, PA 19008
www.masoncrest.com

Printed and bound in the United States of America.

First printing
9 8 7 6 5 4 3 2 1

Series ISBN: 978-1-4222-2874-6
Hardcover ISBN: 978-1-4222-2881-4
ebook ISBN: 978-1-4222-8943-3
Paperback ISBN: 978-1-4222-2989-7

The Library of Congress has cataloged the
       hardcopy format(s) as follows:

              Library of Congress Cataloging-in-Publication Data

Crockett, Kyle A.
  Managing your weight with nutrition / Kyle A. Crockett.
      pages cm. – (Understanding nutrition: a gateway to physical & mental health)
  Audience: 10.
  Audience: Grade 4 to 6.
   ISBN 978-1-4222-2881-4 (hardcover) – ISBN 978-1-4222-2874-6 (series) – ISBN 978-1-4222-2989-7 (paperback) –ISBN 978-1-4222-8943-3 (ebook)
  1. Health–Juvenile literature. 2. Nutrition–Juvenile literature. 3. Diet–Juvenile literature. 4. Weight loss–Juvenile literature. I. Title.
  RA776.5.C76 2014
  613.2–dc23
                        2013009804

Produced by Vestal Creative Services.
www.vestalcreative.com

UNDERSTANDING NUTRITION:
A GATEWAY TO PHYSICAL AND MENTAL HEALTH

Managing Your
Weight with Nutrition

KYLE A. CROCKETT

Mason Crest

CONTENTS

INTRODUCTION
by Dr. Joshua Borus

There are many decisions to make about food. Almost everyone wants to "eat healthy"—but what does that really mean? What is the "right" amount of food and what is a "normal" portion size? Do I need sports drinks if I'm an athlete—or is water okay? Are all "organic" foods healthy? Getting reliable information about nutrition can be confusing. All sorts of restaurants and food makers spend billions of dollars trying to get you to buy their products, often by implying that a food is "good for you" or "healthy." Food packaging has unbiased, standardized nutrition labels, but if you don't know what to look for, they can be hard to understand. Magazine articles and the Internet seem to always have information about the latest fad diets or new "superfoods" but little information you can trust. Finally, everyone's parents, friends, and family have their own views on what is healthy. How are you supposed to make good decisions with all this information when you don't know how to interpret it?

The goal of this series is to arm you with information to help separate what is healthy from not healthy. The books in the series will help you think about things like proper portion size and how eating well can help you stay healthy, improve your mood, and manage your weight. These books will also help you take action. They will let you know some of the changes you can make to keep healthy and how to compare eating options.

Keep in mind a few broad rules:

• First, healthy eating is a lifelong process. Learning to try new foods, preparing foods in healthy ways, and focusing on the big picture are essential parts of that process. Almost no one can keep on a very restrictive diet for a long time or entirely cut out certain groups of foods, so it's best to figure out how to eat healthy in a way that's realistic for you by making a number of small changes.

- Second, a lot of healthy eating hasn't really changed much over the years and isn't that complicated once you know what to look for. The core of a healthy diet is still eating reasonable portions at regular meals. This should be mostly fruits and vegetables, reasonable amounts of proteins, and lots of whole grains, with few fried foods or extra fats. "Junk food" and sweets also have their place—they taste good and have a role in celebrations and other happy events—but they aren't meant to be a cornerstone of your diet!

- Third, avoid drinks with calories in them, beverages like sodas, iced tea, and most juices. Try to make your liquid intake all water and you'll be better off.

- Fourth, eating shouldn't be done mindlessly. Often people will munch while they watch TV or play games because it's something to do or because they're bored rather then because they are hungry. This can lead to lots of extra food intake, which usually isn't healthy. If you are eating, pay attention, so that you are enjoying what you eat and aware of your intake.

- Finally, eating is just one part of the equation. Exercise every day is the other part. Ideally, do an activity that makes you sweat and gets your heart beating fast for an hour a day—but even making small decisions like taking stairs instead of elevators or walking home from school instead of driving make a difference.

After you read this book, don't stop. Find out more about healthy eating. Choosemyplate.gov is a great Internet resource from the U.S. government that can be trusted to give good information; www.hsph.harvard.edu/nutritionsource is a webpage from the Harvard School of Public Health where scientists sort through all the data about food and nutrition and distill it into easy-to-understand messages. Your doctor or nurse can also help you learn more about making good decisions. You might also want to meet with a nutritionist to get more information about healthy living.

Food plays an important role in social events, informs our cultural heritage and traditions, and is an important part of our daily lives. It's not just how we fuel our bodies; it's also but how we nourish our spirit. Learn how to make good eating decisions and build healthy eating habits—and you'll have increased long-term health, both physically and psychologically.

So get started now!

1

How Much
Is Too Much?

Eating is probably one of the most important parts of your day. After all, if you didn't eat, you couldn't do much of anything else. Eating food is what keeps you going. It gives you the energy you need to play sports and go to school. Without it, you wouldn't be able to learn or have a good time with your friends. You would get tired and very sick.

You have to eat more than once a day. A good breakfast in the morning helps you wake up and gives you energy. Then you eat lunch to keep you going. In the evening you eat dinner. You might eat snacks in between all those meals too. That can add up to a lot of food!

Eating is fun. Cooking and eating food with other people is a great part of life. But sometimes we go overboard. We like eating too much. Or we eat too many unhealthy foods. Eating too much and eating too many unhealthy foods can result in an unhealthy weight. And that leads to getting sick.

Why Do I Care About Weight?

Lots and lots of people weigh too much. People who weigh a little too much are overweight. People who are very heavy are obese. About a third of all young people are either overweight or obese. That means that one out of every three kids weighs too much. So it's not weird to be overweight or obese!

But just because a lot of people weigh too much doesn't mean being overweight or obese isn't a problem. In fact, it means it's a very serious health problem. It means we should work even harder to help people get to a healthy weight!

When people weigh too much, their bodies don't work as well. They get tired more easily. They get sick.

Weighing too much might make you feel bad about yourself too. Being overweight doesn't mean you're a bad person. Or that you're ugly. But some overweight kids get teased or feel like they're too fat. They don't feel good about themselves.

Young people who are overweight sometimes get sick more often than kids who aren't. They're more likely to get asthma. Or have trouble sleeping. Or get stomachaches a lot. Or have trouble moving.

When you weigh too much, you might get seriously sick. One of the biggest dangers of being overweight or obese is diabetes.

Diabetes is a disease where your body doesn't use sugar the way it should. Insulin is a chemical in your blood that helps your body use sugar so you can have energy for moving and doing things. When someone has diabetes, something goes wrong with the insulin. One type of diabetes is caused partly by weighing too much.

Years ago, young people didn't get diabetes very often. Not many kids were overweight or obese. But now, more and more young people weigh too much. Now, more and more kids have diabetes too, which can make life much harder for them.

Eating too much unhealthy food can leave you feeling tired and sick more often than you should. Overweight people can have many different health problems such as trouble sleeping, diabetes, or heart disease.

Young people who weight too much are more likely to be overweight when they're adults too. And being overweight when you're an adult leads to even more health problems. Overweight adults might get heart disease. They might get diabetes, even if they didn't have it as a kid. They might have trouble moving around.

The good news is that you can do something about it! If you're overweight or obese, it doesn't mean you always have to be. You can stay a healthy weight by eating right and getting exercise.

More About Diabetes

There are actually two kinds of diabetes. One is called Type 1 diabetes. It is usually passed from parents to children. Type 1 diabetes doesn't really have much to do with a person's weight. Someone who is a healthy weight can get Type 1 diabetes. People with Type 1 get it when they are kids and have to give themselves shots of insulin.

The other kind of diabetes is Type 2 diabetes. Being overweight or obese often causes this kind of diabetes. People with Type 2 diabetes usually don't have to get shots, but they do have to watch what they eat. They have to exercise, and lose weight. They are more likely to get sick later on than people without diabetes. For example, they could get heart disease or kidney failure. It's much better to avoid getting Type 2 diabetes in the first place!

Body Mass Index

You can't always look in the mirror and tell whether you weigh too much. Everyone's body is different. Some people have heavier bones. Some have more muscle. Some are tall, short, and everything in between.

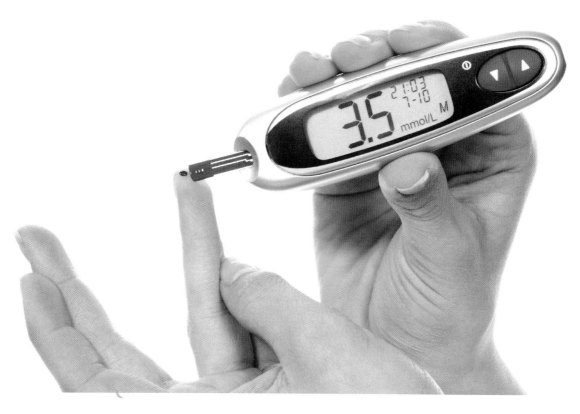

Many people with diabetes have to test their blood sugar levels every day. They have to make sure that their amount of sugar in their blood isn't too low or too high.

Doctors have come up with a way to tell if a person weighs too much. They call it the Body Mass Index, or BMI. BMI depends on how tall you are and how much you weigh. It's a number. Everyone has a BMI. Your BMI can tell you if you're overweight or obese—or if you're underweight or just right.

Doctors have BMI charts that tell them whether or not a person weighs the right amount. Someone with a very low BMI is underweight. She should weigh more to be healthy. Someone with a very high BMI is overweight. He should weigh less to be healthy.

There are special BMI charts for people between two and twenty. The special charts are called BMI-by-age charts. BMI works a little differently for kids than for adults.

If you're worried about your weight, go to your doctor. Ask her to figure out your BMI. Then you can talk to her about what you should do if your BMI is too low or too high.

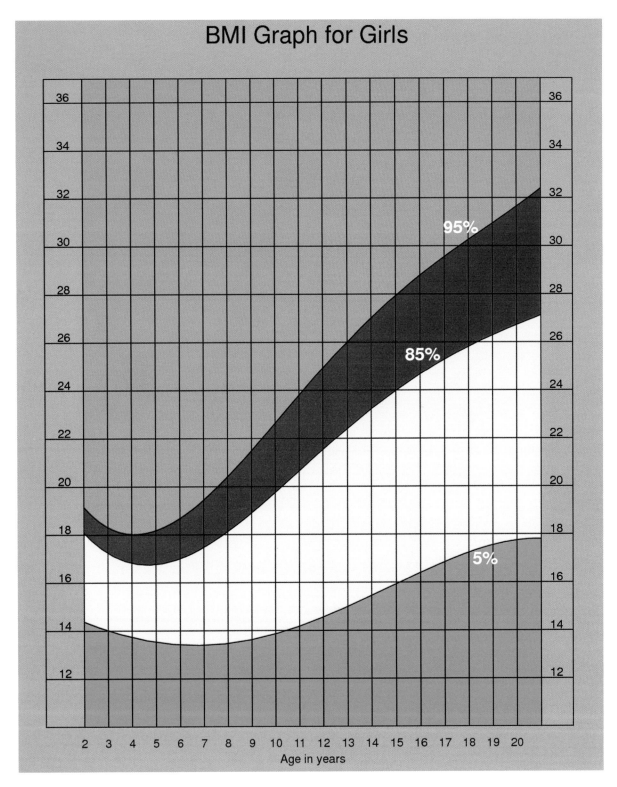

BMI Graph for Girls

Age in years

This chart can help you figure out whether your BMI puts you in the underweight (green), normal (yellow), overweight (red), or obese (blue) category. The chart for boys is on page 16.

BMI Formula

If you want to figure out your own BMI, here's what you need to do:

1. Weigh yourself and write it down.
2. Measure how tall you are in inches (height) and write it down.
3. Use this equation. (Ask an adult to help if you can't figure out the math.)

   BMI = weight x 703/(height x height)

4. Once you figure out your BMI number, find where it falls on a BMI chart. Be sure to use a BMI-by-age chart if you're under twenty.

But BMI isn't always the best way to tell if you're overweight. Some people are just heavier than others—but not because they have too much fat. Let's say Francisco and Nick go to the school nurse to find out their BMIs. They're both boys, and they are both the same height. Francisco weighs more than Nick, though. He has a higher BMI. Francisco's BMI says he's overweight.

But Francisco plays a lot of sports. He has more muscles than Nick. Muscles are heavy. Francisco has a higher BMI because he has more muscles. And having more muscles is not unhealthy like fat. So Francisco probably isn't overweight.

Just Right

Figuring out if you're a healthy weight can be confusing!

Lots of TV shows, movies, and video games tell us we should be skinny. Actors, musicians, and other stars are often very thin. People today think skinny is beautiful, especially for girls. When we see those actors, we feel like we should be very skinny too.

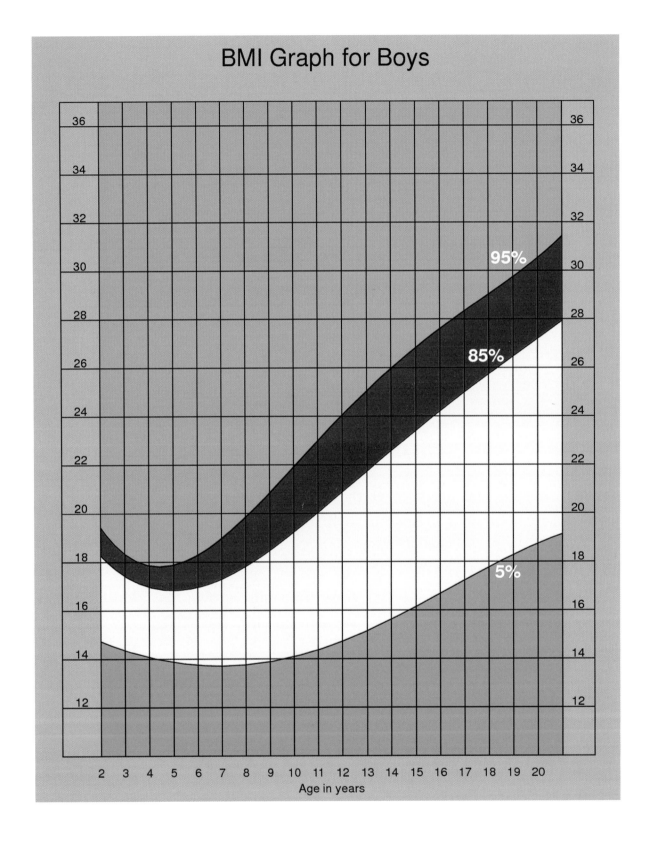

BMI Graph for Boys

95%

85%

5%

Age in years

That isn't true, though. If you don't weigh enough, you might be just as unhealthy as someone who weighs too much.

There are lots of people telling us to eat too much, too. Think of all the junk food ads you see on TV. Those ads are meant to make you hungry for foods that could make you overweight. Or maybe your friends and family are always snacking. It's easy to go along with whatever people around you are doing.

Each person has a different weight that is healthy. In the end, everyone is different. One twelve-year-old who weighs a hundred pounds might be overweight. Another might be just fine. And another might be underweight. It depends on how tall each one is and how much muscle or fat each has.

So don't be quick to tell yourself you're too fat or too skinny. You might be absolutely normal for your age. The best thing to do is talk to your doctor if you're worried. Find out what's right for you!

2

How Nutrition Affects Your Weight

Your weight depends on two things. One is how much exercise you get. The other is how much and what kind of food you eat.

Food and Your Body

Everything you eat does something to your body. Food can do good things for you. And food can do not-so-good things for you.

What Are Nutrients?

Nutrients are things like vitamins and minerals that our bodies need to grow and live. We get nutrients from foods.

For example, let's say you drink a soda. It has a lot of sugar in it. Sugar gives you a lot of energy for a short time. At first, you may feel like running around. Then you get tired and want to sleep. You might even have a headache. That's one way soda affects you. You might also get a cavity in one of your teeth from the sugar, if you drink enough soda. Cavities are caused by sugar. Soda doesn't seem like it's very good for your body, does it?

Now let's say you eat a stir-fry with lots of veggies and brown rice. You feel full but you also feel like you have a lot of energy. The energy lasts for a long time, until you're ready to eat again. Eating all those veggies and rice also gives you lots of **nutrients**. Vegetables have vitamins like Vitamin A and C. They have minerals like iron and calcium. Those things help you grow up strong and healthy.

Food can also make our bodies store fat. When we eat too much food, we gain weight because our bodies are storing fat. When we eat too much of the wrong foods, we gain weight too.

Calories and Too Much Food

You might think that calories are something bad—but your body needs calories. Calories are a way to measure the energy in your food. A food with 500 calories has a lot more energy than a food with 50 calories. Your body needs energy to work right. So it needs calories.

Your body uses calories all the time. It uses calories to pump your heart. And to breath. And to walk, run, and jump. Everything you do burns calories.

Calories aren't bad for you. Everyone needs calories to live. If we didn't eat calories, we would get sick and eventually die.

But eating too many calories can make us sick too.

Everything we do—from walking to thinking to riding a bike—burns calories. To lose weight, you have to burn more calories than you eat and drink. Exercising is the best way to burn extra calories that you wouldn't burn just sitting around.

How Nutrition Affects Your Weight **21**

Most people need to eat between 1,600 and 2,500 calories a day to be healthy. People often say that humans need 2,000 calories every day, but everyone is different. Some people need more and some people need less. A boy who is tall and has a lot of muscles needs to eat more calories. A girl who is short probably needs fewer calories.

Two big things affect your weight. The first thing is exercise. The second thing is calories. When you eat more calories than your body needs, you gain weight. If you eat fewer calories than your body needs, you lose weight.

Exercise can make you lose weight too. When we move, we use up calories. So when we move a lot, we burn even more calories! If you're trying to lose weight, you can exercise to burn up the extra calories you eat.

Good Calories

We need calories to live, but some calories are better than others. The best calories are in foods that have other things in them, like vitamins and minerals.

Vitamins and minerals help your body work right. They help you digest food. They help you see. They help you fight sickness.

Our bodies can't make all the vitamins and minerals they need. We have to get vitamins and minerals from food. Some foods don't have many vitamins and minerals. Some foods have a lot.

Fruits and vegetables and whole grains have a lot of vitamins and minerals. So do meat and dairy. They also have calories. But those calories come with lots of good vitamins and minerals. They're healthy.

Other foods don't have many vitamins and minerals. Processed foods don't usually have a lot of vitamins and minerals. Processed foods are made in factories. Chips, cookies, boxed macaroni and cheese, and ice cream are all processed foods. Those kinds of food have a lot of calories in them. But they don't have many vitamins and minerals. Instead, they have lots of sugar or salt. Your body needs a little sugar and salt. But not too much. Processed foods have too much.

The best foods to eat have some calories and a lot of vitamins and minerals. Those are healthy foods.

Choosing fruits or vegetables over high-calorie foods is a great way to start eating healthy. Fruits and vegetables have lots of vitamins and minerals that help to keep you at your best.

Calories in Foods

There are lots of lists online that tell you how many calories are in the food you eat. Here are a few foods and how many calories are in each one.

- 1 banana = 105 calories
- 1 plain bagel = 360 calories
- 8 oz. low fat chocolate milk = 158 calories
- 1 cup whole wheat spaghetti = 176 calories
- 1 cup raw carrots = 50 calories
- 6 fast-food chicken nuggets = 360 calories
- 1 cup vanilla ice cream = 273 calories

Unhealthy foods are foods that have a lot of calories and not many vitamins and minerals. You should only eat those foods once in a while.

Healthy Food

Lots of people groan when they hear the words "healthy food." Young people, especially, often think healthy fruits and vegetables taste bad.

That's not true, though. Just about anyone can learn to like healthy foods. And it's really important to eat them. Adults don't tell you to eat healthy foods because they want to be mean or annoying. They care about you. They want you to eat healthy foods because they want *you* to be healthy. If you think about it, you want the same thing. No one really wants to be sick. No one likes feeling tired all the time. Being strong and healthy means you can do better at sports and in school. It means you'll feel happier. You'll look better. Eating healthy foods just makes sense.

500 cal
A large order of McDonald's french fries

300 cal
A packet of potato crisps

111 cal
half-cup of mashed potatoes with milk and butter

220 cal
white baked potato, with skin

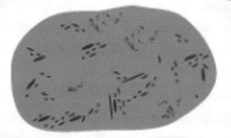

117 cal
sweet baked potato with skin

145 cal
white baked potato, without skin

144 cal
Newmedium piece of candied sweet potato

A baked potato can be a healthy, tasty snack that gives you plenty of energy. Fries, however, have many more calories because they are cooked in oil and covered in salt.

You don't have to stop enjoying your favorite foods in order to lose weight or feel better. Making sweets and snacks a "sometimes food" is a great way to begin losing weight.

Healthy foods are fruits and vegetables. Whole grains (like brown rice, whole-wheat bread, and oatmeal) are healthy. So are dairy and meat. You also stay healthy for a long time if you eat healthy foods.

When you eat too many unhealthy foods, you can get seriously sick. And you might gain a lot of weight, which also can make you sick. Eating a lot of unhealthy foods for a long time can lead to heart disease, diabetes, a **stroke**, or sleep problems. That's a lot of problems just from eating unhealthy food!

What Is a Stroke?

A **stroke** is when blood flow in your brain is interrupted, so that brain cells die because they don't get oxygen. When this happens, parts of your body will no longer work normally. You might not be able to speak or move. A stroke can also cause death.

A List of Healthy Foods

Here's a short list of just some foods that are good for you to eat:

- fresh apples
- brown rice
- carrot sticks
- low-fat milk
- oatmeal
- raisins
- smoothies
- whole grain crackers
- baked chicken
- cherry tomatoes

3

Ways to Change Your Diet to Lose Weight

Talking about eating healthy is one thing. Doing it is another. First, you have to know what's healthy and what isn't. Then you have to make choices.

It's not always easy. But there are lots of simple things you can do to eat healthy. All those simple things will add up to a healthy diet!

FRUITS Fuel Up With Fruits at Meals or Snacks

Oranges, pears, berries, watermelon, peaches, raisins, and applesauce (without extra sugar) are just a few of the great choices. Make sure your juice is 100% fruit juice.

VEGETABLES Color Your Plate With Great-Tasting Veggies

Try to eat more dark-green, red, and orange vegetables, and beans and peas.

You should eat more fruit and vegetables than any other kind of food. Fruit and vegetables are always a healthy food choice because they don't have the fat, sugar, and salt that many unhealthy foods do.

Deciding to Lose Weight

Maybe you're thinking about losing weight. You might look in the mirror and think, "I'm so fat, I'm ugly."

That's not a good way to think. A lot of people are overweight or obese. That doesn't mean they're bad people or that they're ugly. They should think about losing weight because it will make them healthier. Not because being fat is considered ugly.

And a lot of people think they're an unhealthy weight when they're not. There's a lot of pressure to be skinny. Being skinny isn't always healthy either. You want to be the right weight for you. And you might already be the right weight.

The best thing to do is to talk to a doctor. She can help you figure out if you're the right weight or not. She'll measure your height and weight. She'll figure out your BMI. Then she'll look at a chart and tell you if you're a good weight. She might say you're just fine and not to change anything. She might say you need to gain weight. She might say you need to lose weight.

If you need to lose weight, a doctor can give you some tips. He can help you figure out how to exercise more. He can also help you come up with a plan for making good food choices.

Eat Fruits and Veggies

Probably the best thing you can do for your health is eat more fruits and vegetables. They have a lot of good vitamins and minerals.

Fresh and frozen fruits and vegetables are the best. They have lots of vitamins like Vitamins A and C. And minerals like iron. Fiber from fresh and frozen veggies help keep your digestive system healthy.

Canned fruits and veggies aren't always the best choices. Canned food sometimes has a lot of sugar and salt added to it. Check the label on the can. Read the ingredient list. If it lists sodium, that's salt. If it lists high fructose corn syrup, that's sugar. Stick to cans that mostly have just fruits and vegetables, not extra stuff.

How Important Is Exercising?

Getting exercise is another important part of being healthy. It keeps your body working the way it should. It makes you stronger. And it helps you lose weight if you need to.

Today, kids spend about 45 hours a week in front of computers, TVs, and video games. The only thing they do more is sleep! All that time in front of screens means less time for exercising.

Taking a walk counts as exercising. So does playing a sport. Or playing with a pet. Make it a goal to spend less time in front of the TV, and more time moving around!

Try to eat lots of fruits and vegetables. Every meal should have some. A good rule is to make half of your plate fruits and vegetables. If you eat a turkey sandwich for lunch, you should also have a salad or carrot sticks or sweet potato fries. And an apple or orange. Eat as many colors as you can. Every color is good for a different part of your body. Have you ever heard that carrots are good for your eyes? It's true—all orange fruits and vegetables are good for your eyes. Other colors help other things. Eat them all for a totally healthy body.

Whole Grains

Grains are the seeds of grass plants. Rice is a giant grass. So are oats. And wheat. When you eat whole grains, you're eating the entire seed.

We make lots of food out of grains. Bread is made out of wheat. Pasta is made out of wheat too. Oatmeal is made out of oats. Cereal is made out of wheat, corn, and rice.

Food made from grains that aren't whole grain are made from only a part of the seed. Factories take out the other parts. That leaves the flour looking whiter. White bread and regular pasta are made from white flour.

Eat Your Colors

Every color of fruit and vegetable is good for a different part of your body. You should eat all of them to keep your whole body healthy. Green is good for your bones; that's because green things like kale and green beans have calcium in them, just like milk does. Brown and white (like potatoes and turnips) are good for digestion. Blue and purple (like blueberries and eggplants) are good for your brain. Red (like peppers and apples) are good for your heart. Orange and yellow foods like carrots and pineapple are good for your eyes.

Instead Of:	Choose Whole Grains:
White rice	Brown rice, wild rice, quinoa
White flour	Whole-wheat flour
White bread or wheat bread	100% Whole-grain bread
Noodles, pasta, spaghetti, macaroni	Whole-wheat pasta or whole-grain noodles
Flour tortillas	Whole-grain tortillas and whole-corn tortillas that do not have "lime" in the ingredient list
Crackers	Whole-grain crackers
Degermed cornmeal	Whole-grain cornmeal

Whole grains are much healthier than foods made with white flour. Try switching white bread, flour tortillas, and other foods made with white flour for whole-grain foods. Whole-grain foods have more nutrients than foods made from only part of the grain.

Whole-grain foods are usually darker. Brown rice is a whole grain. Whole-wheat bread and whole-wheat pasta are brown.

Foods made out of the entire grain seed are much healthier for you. That's because the parts of the seeds that are removed to make white flour and white rice actually have a lot of good vitamins and minerals in them. That's why whole grains are a part of a good diet.

Eat as many whole grains as possible. Anytime you eat whole grains, you're getting lots of good nutrition.

Nutrition Facts

Serving Size 1 cup (228g)
Servings Per Container about 2

① Serving Size

Amount Per Serving

Calories 250	Calories from Fat 110

② Amount of Calories

	% Daily Value*
Total Fat 12g	**18%**
Saturated Fat 3g	**15%**
Trans Fat 3g	
Cholesterol 30mg	**10%**
Sodium 470mg	**20%**
Total Carbohydrate 31g	**10%**
Dietary Fiber 0g	**0%**
Sugars 5g	
Proteins 5g	
Vitamin A	4%
Vitamin C	2%
Calcium	20%
Iron	4%

③ Limit These Nutrients

④ Get Enough of These Nutrients

⑤ Percent (%) Daily Value

* Percent Daily Values are based on a 2,000 calorie diet. Your Daily Values may be higher or lower depending on your calorie needs:

⑥ Footnote With Daily Values (DVs)

	Calories:	2,000	2,500
Total Fat	Less than	65g	80g
Saturated Fat	Less than	20g	25g
Cholesterol	Less than	300mg	300mg
Sodium	Less than	2,400mg	2,400mg
Total Carbohydrate		300g	375g
Dietary Fiber		25g	30g

Reading Food Labels

All packaged food has a food label. Part of the label lists the ingredients. Don't eat foods that list "high fructose corn syrup" as one of the first ingredients. Or salt or glucose, fructose, or dextrose (all of those are sugars). You can also read the nutrition table. That shows how many calories the food has. And what nutrients it has. For each nutrient, the table shows a percent. That percent is how much of a nutrient you're eating compared to how much you need in one day. Stay away from foods that have really high numbers for sodium (salt). Stay away from high numbers for carbohydrates (sugar) too. High numbers for calcium, protein, and vitamins are good, though, so try to include more of those foods in your diet every day.

Cut Down on Salt and Sugar

Foods with lots of sugar and salt cause weight gain. They have a lot of calories in them. And they don't have very many vitamins or minerals.

Lots of things that come in wrappers are in this category. The grocery store has lots of salty things. Potato chips and crackers have a lot of salt. So do frozen meals. And canned soup.

Grocery stores have even more foods with sugar. Cookies have a lot of sugar. And candy. And baked goods.

A lot of foods have something called high fructose corn syrup. High fructose corn syrup is a kind of sugar made from corn. That doesn't mean that it's good for you. High fructose corn syrup is very sweet. Eating too much of it can make you gain weight.

High fructose corn syrup is in lots of things. It's in cereal. It's in yogurt. It's in applesauce and jam. It's even in ketchup.

It's okay to eat sugar and salt sometimes. But if you save sugary and salty foods for special occasions, you'll be less likely to gain weight. If you stop eating so much of them, you might lose a few pounds.

Drink Water

It's not just foods that make you gain weight. Don't forget about drinks! Lots of drinks have way too much sugar. Soda, especially, has a lot. Soda usually has high fructose corn syrup. Other drinks have sugar too. Lots of juice drinks do, like juice boxes. Sports drinks have a lot of sugar as well.

You can gain weight by drinking these kinds of things. To lose weight, cut out soda. Only drink juice that says it's 100 percent fruit juice, with no extra sugar added. Even better, drink water whenever you're thirsty. Water doesn't have any extra sugar. And it doesn't have calories!

Healthy Snacks

Snack time might be making you gain weight. If you reach for Oreos, chips, or ice cream for a snack, think twice. Snacks sometimes just add calories you don't need.

But snacks can help keep you healthy. They're a good way to keep you going during the day. If you choose the right snacks, you add vitamins and minerals to your diet.

Pick snacks with fruit, veggies, dairy, and whole grains. A piece of fresh fruit is a good snack. Or whole-wheat crackers and cheese. Or yogurt. Or carrot sticks and hummus.

Portion Control

A lot of weight gain comes from just eating too much. Even eating too many healthy foods can lead to gaining weight.

We're used to eating a lot. Often, people eat until they're uncomfortably full. Whenever that happens, you're eating a lot of extra, unneeded calories.

A good rule is to eat until you're almost full, but not quite. As you digest what you ate, you'll feel fuller. You'll feel better after a meal where you've eaten the right amount. Too much food makes you feel tired and unable to move. The right portions keep you going until your next meal.

Simple Weight-Loss Rules

If you want to lose weight, remember these simple rules:

- Eat more fruits, vegetables, and whole grains.
- Eat less sugar and salt.
- Drink more water and less soda.
- Eat healthy snacks.

Eating right will help you take off unhealthy pounds. If you exercise, you'll lose even more. And if you make healthy eating and exercise a habit, you'll be healthier your whole life!

What Not to Do

There are healthy ways to lose weight. There are also unhealthy ways. It's very unhealthy to just stop eating. Don't skip any meals. People need to eat food. Otherwise our bodies don't work. Young people who are still growing especially need to eat. If you stop eating enough food, you'll lose weight—but you'll also mess up your growth. And you'll feel sick. Don't follow special diets either. There are diets that tell you only to eat grapefruit for every meal. Or to mostly eat meat. They might help you lose weight, but they're not healthy. Eating right and exercising are the only healthy ways to lose weight.

4

Healthy Snacks

Losing weight is one thing. Staying a healthy weight is another. Lots of people lose weight. And then they gain it back again.

That's because they don't know the good habits they need to follow. A lot of these habits are the same as losing weight. You should always eat fruits and veggies. You should drink more water than soda. You should snack healthy.

You want to be healthy for a lifetime. Not just while you're losing weight!

Getting your friends and family involved in healthy eating can be one of the best ways to make sure you don't go back to making unhealthy food choices.

Choosing Wisely in School

At school, you might be tempted to eat french fries for lunch everyday. Or get a soda from the vending machine after school.

Be smart! Just because you're at school doesn't mean you can forget about eating healthy. Choose the best options for breakfast and lunch. Always eat fruits and vegetables. And pick whole-grain bread, pasta, and rice if you can.

If you have to get a snack from the vending machine, some choices are better than others. Get 100 percent fruit juice, not soda. Choose whole grain pretzels, not super salty potato chips. And if you bring lunch from home, don't trade your celery and oranges for candy and cookies!

Get Your Family on Board

If your family doesn't have very healthy eating habits, it can make it harder for you to form good habits. But chances are, if you talk to your family, they'll be willing to help you. Make a grocery list with healthy foods you want to try. Find new healthier recipes online and in cookbooks. Offer to help prepare healthy meals. You can help make your entire family healthier!

Don't Pay Attention to the TV

TV can be dangerous to our health in a few different ways. If you're watching TV, you're not moving very much. That's not good for your body. Make sure you take some time off from TV and get some exercise. Exercise burns calories, and it helps keep your body from putting on weight.

TV is also bad for us in other ways. It's very good at telling us to eat unhealthy foods. Think of all the food commercials you see. Sugary cereal. Cookies. Soda. Candy. Once you see a commercial, you know that food. You'll recognize it when you go to the grocery store. And you'll want to eat it.

Description, Analysis is based on one Burger	Calories	Fat (g)
Burger King, Hamburger	333	15
Burger King, Cheeseburger	380	20
Burger King, Cheeseburger, Whopper Jr	460	27
Burger King, Hamburger, Whopper	678	37
Burger King, Cheeseburger, Whopper	790	48
Burger King, Cheeseburger, Double Whopper	1061	68
McDonald's Hamburger	265	10
McDonald's Cheeseburger	313	14
McDonald's Hamburger, Quarter Pounder	417	20
McDonald's Cheeseburger, Big Mac	563	33
McDonald's Cheeseburger, Quarter Pounder, double	734	45
Wendy's, Hamburger, jr	284	10
Wendy's, Hamburger, classic single	464	23
Wendy's, Cheeseburger, classic single	522	27
Wendy's, Hamburger, Big Bacon Classic	570	29
Wendy's, Cheeseburger, classic double	747	44
White Castle, Hamburger, Slyder	140	7
White Castle, Cheeseburger	160	9
White Castle, Cheeseburger, double	290	18
White Castle, Cheeseburger, bacon, double	360	23

Fast-food commercials may make you want to take a trip to the drive-thru, but remember that most fast food is high in calories and fat. One meal at a fast-food restaurant can be as many as 3,000 calories, much more than you need to eat in a whole day.

There are lots of commercials for unhealthy foods. There aren't very many commercials for healthy foods. So learn to stop paying so much attention to television. Think for yourself!

Make Time for Meals

One habit lots of people have is eating somewhere besides the kitchen or dining room table. We eat in the car. Or while walking. Or in front of the TV. Or at a restaurant.

When people eat in front of the TV, they might end up eating more than if they weren't watching TV. If they eat in rush, they grab whatever's easiest and quickest. That's often a packaged food that has lots of salt and sugar. Or maybe your family stops at the fast food drive-through and gets dinner to eat in the car. That's usually not as healthy as eating at home.

Make time to eat. The best thing to do is eat at home at your own table. That way, you're paying attention to what you're eating. You can decide what the healthiest choices are for each meal. Cook meals from scratch. (Don't just eat frozen dinners.) Cooking will give you time to hang out with your family. And families that eat together at the dinner table are often healthier.

Think Positive

Sometimes the hardest part of healthy eating is learning how to do it. When you first start eating healthy food, you want to eat all the stuff you normally eat, like sugar. It's hard to change. It's easy to get discouraged.

But think positive. List all the reasons why you want to lose weight. Maybe you want to be able to run faster. You want to look better in your jeans. You want to be healthier. Think about those reasons whenever you get tempted to give up.

Losing weight doesn't happen over night. But if you stick with your new healthy eating habits long enough, you'll start to see that you're looking thinner. You'll start to feel better. Then you have really good reasons to keep eating healthy!

Working on losing weight can be tough when you think negatively. Watching the number of calories you eat and making heatlhy food choices can be difficult sometimes, but stick with it and you'll feel better about yourself.

And don't give up when you finally reach a healthy weight. Keep following all those healthy rules you already know. You'll be stronger, happier, and healthier!

Find Out More

ONLINE

BMI for Children and Teens
www.cdc.gov/healthyweight/assessing/bmi/childrens_bmi/about_childrens_bmi.html

Healthy Weight Loss Guide
kidshealth.org/teen/managing_weight_center/tools/healthy_weight_module.html

Kids Health: Managing Your Weight
kidshealth.org/teen/centers/weight_center.html

President's Council on Fitness, Sports, and Nutrition
www.fitness.gov/eat-healthy/how-to-eat-healthy/

IN BOOKS

Bickerstaff, Linda. *Nutrition Sense: Counting Calories, Figuring Out Fats, and Eating Balanced Meals.* New York: Rosen Publishing, 2008.

Gay, Kathlyn. *The Scoop on What to Eat: What You Should Know About Diet and Nutrition.* Berkeley Heights, N.J.: Enslow Publishers, 2009.

Hawley, Ella. *Exploring Food and Nutrition.* New York: Powerkids Press, 2012

Index

About the Author & Consultant

Kyle A. Crockett is a freelance writer whose work can be found in print and online. His writing for young people has focused on topics ranging from health to economics.

Dr. Borus graduated from the Harvard Medical School and the Harvard School of Public Health. He completed a residency in Pediatrics and then served as Chief Resident at Floating Hospital for Children at Tufts Medical Center before completing a fellowship in Adolescent Medicine at Boston Children's Hospital. He is currently an attending physician in the Division of Adolescent and Young Adult Medicine at Boston Children's Hospital and an Instructor of Pediatrics at Harvard Medical School.

Picture Credits